Mr Football

by

Janet Olearski

HELBLING LANGUAGES

www.helblinglanguages.com

Mr Football
by Janet Olearski
© HELBLING LANGUAGES 2008

First published 2009

ISBN 978-3-85272-159-0

The publishers would like to thank the following for their kind permission to reproduce the following photographs and other copyright material: **Corbis** p94; **Dreamstime** p7 (soccer team); ©**iStockphoto.com** p7 (fast food); **Shelleycat, Flickr.com** p8 (pennant); **Shutterstock** p8.

Series editor Maria Cleary
Written by Janet Olearski
Illustrated by Marzia Sanfilippo
Activities by Janet Olearski
Design and layout by BNC comunicazione
Printed by Athesia

About this Book

For the Student

🎧 Listen to all of the story and do some activities on your Audio CD

💬 Talk about the story

beat° When you see the green dot you can check the word in the glossary

For the Teacher

Go to our Readers Resource site for information on using readers and downloadable Resource Sheets, photocopiable Worksheets, Answer Keys and Tapescripts.

Plus free sample tracks from the story.
www.helblingreaders.com

For lots of great ideas on using Graded Readers consult Reading Matters, the Teacher's Guide to using Helbling Readers.

Level 3 Structures

Present continuous for future	Cardinal / ordinal numbers
Present perfect	*One / ones*
Present perfect versus past simple	Reflexive pronouns
Should / shouldn't (advice and obligation)	Indefinite pronouns
Must / should	
Need to / have to	*Too* plus adjective
Will	*Not* plus adjective plus *enough*
	Relative pronouns *who, which* and *that*
Ever / never	Prepositions of time, place and movement
Would like	
So do I / neither do I	
Question tags	

Structures from lower levels are also included

Contents

Meet the Author

Hello, Janet, can you tell us a little about yourself?

I was born in London and grew up there. I studied languages at the University of Edinburgh in Scotland. I trained as● an English teacher and I taught English in Italy and a number of other countries. A few years ago I got a job in Abu Dhabi in the United Arab Emirates, and that's where I am now.

Where do you get the ideas for your stories?

I have always loved writing and I am constantly looking for interesting news items● that I can use in my stories. I keep cuttings● from newspapers and I carry a notebook with me at all times so that I can immediately write down any stories that come into my head or that people tell me.

How did you think of this story?

In my school and university holidays, I had a lot of part-time● jobs, including one – which was not so pleasant – in a fish and chip shop. As for football... well, I don't play it myself, but I love to watch a good game. I've found that wherever you go in the world, you will always find someone who loves football as much as my hero Gary does.

Why did you write this story?

I wanted to show that sometimes we have to work hard to get the things we want in life. The rewards● are great when we make the effort.

Glossary

- **cuttings:** stories you cut from a newspaper
- **items:** (here) stories
- **part-time:** not a full day or week
- **rewards:** prizes etc., for doing something well
- **trained as:** learned to be

Before Reading

1 **Look quickly at the pictures in the book and answer the questions.**

   a) Who is the main character?
      1 ☐ a famous footballer
      2 ☐ a teenager
      3 ☐ a football coach

   b) What kind of story is it?
      1 ☐ Human Interest
      2 ☐ Detective Story
      3 ☐ Love Story

2 **Look at the chapter titles on the Contents page. Work with a partner or in a small group. Make up a short story. Use the chapter titles as ideas to guide you.**

3 **Look at the pictures below. Describe what you see.**

a)

b)

4 **Which job is better? Give reasons.**

Before Reading

1 Match the words to the pictures.

a) whistle   b) goalkeeper   c) trophy   d) mug

e) pennants   f) saucer   g) fist   h) overcoat

1
2
3
4

5
6
7
8

2 Now use these words to complete the sentences below.

a) The cat ate its food from a .... on the kitchen floor.

b) Gary's dad filled his .... with hot tea.

c) You don't need to wear an .... when the weather is warm.

d) Mr Hussain the referee blew his ....

e) Gary punched his .... in the air.

f) The .... jumped with his hands stretched out and tried to catch the ball.

g) The mayor presented a .... to the winning team.

h) Gary covered the walls of his room with .... from all the famous international clubs.

3 **Listen to these descriptions of the characters and number the pictures.**

a)

b)

c)

d)

4 The hero of Mr Football is a boy called Gary. Look at this picture of him. What do you think he is like? Write down questions you would like to ask him. Ask and answer with a partner.

Before Reading

1 **On a scale of 1 to 5 (1 = I don't agree at all; 5 = I agree completely) how far do you agree with the following statements?**

a) You don't need to be clever to be a footballer.
   1 ☐   2 ☐   3 ☐   4 ☐   5 ☐

b) Children usually grow up to be like their parents.
   1 ☐   2 ☐   3 ☐   4 ☐   5 ☐

c) People pay more attention to boys than to girls.
   1 ☐   2 ☐   3 ☐   4 ☐   5 ☐

d) We should always help our friends – even when our friends behave badly.
   1 ☐   2 ☐   3 ☐   4 ☐   5 ☐

e) Girls shouldn't play football.
   1 ☐   2 ☐   3 ☐   4 ☐   5 ☐

f) We understand the value of something better when we have to pay for it with our own money.
   1 ☐   2 ☐   3 ☐   4 ☐   5 ☐

g) When things go wrong, we should give up and do something new.
   1 ☐   2 ☐   3 ☐   4 ☐   5 ☐

2 **Choose one of the statements and discuss with a partner.**

3 **Who is your favourite footballer? Here are the names of some world-famous footballers. Do you know where they are from? Match the footballers with the countries they come from.**

a) ☐ Pele   1 Northern Ireland
b) ☐ Diego Maradona   2 France
c) ☐ Michel Platini   3 Mozambique
d) ☐ Eusebio   4 Brazil
e) ☐ George Best   5 Argentina

4 What would you do in these situations? Discuss with your partner and then tell the class.

a) You want to buy something but you haven't got any money.

b) You think you are going to win a prize, but your friend gets the prize instead of you.

c) You are in a shop and you see someone stealing something.

d) Someone from your school is causing you a lot of trouble.

e) You are late for an important exam.

5 These pictures tell the story of one of the characters in the story. Work with a partner. Tell the story in your own words.

THE MAD FOOTBALLER

Gary watched as Matt gave the ball a powerful° kick. It rose high into the air. A tall blond-haired boy from the Manning High team ran across the football pitch°. He took control of the ball as it landed, but Gary was already there beside him. He raced past the blond player and caught the ball with his feet. There was a cry from the crowd°.

'Gary! Gary! Gary!' they chanted°.

The score was nil° nil. There were just five minutes to go before the end of the match. Gary knew that every second counted.

From the edge of the pitch, Karen screamed, 'Come on, Gary. Come on!'

'We'll never do it,' said Joe. He was standing next to Karen in the middle of the shouting crowd of schoolchildren. 'Manning High has the best players. Gary can't beat Rick. Rick's much stronger.'

Rick was running alongside° Gary. He intercepted° the ball and kicked it in the opposite direction. The crowd gave another roar.

'See!' said Joe. 'Manning High has got the ball now. We'll never win.'

A girl with long dark hair pushed through the crowd to join Karen and Joe.

'Hurry up, Laura, you're late,' said Karen.

'Sorry,' said Laura, 'I ran all the way from college. What's happening?'

Before Karen could answer, Mr Hussain the referee° blew the whistle.

Glossary

- **alongside:** next to
- **chanted:** sang or shouted
- **crowd:** large group of people
- **intercepted:** stopped; caught
- **nil:** zero
- **pitch:** place where people play football or other sports
- **powerful:** strong
- **referee:** person who makes sure the players follow the rules

'Is that it? Is the match finished?' said Laura.

'No, there's a free kick for us,' said Joe.

'What's that?' said Laura.

Joe rolled his eyes● and looked at Karen.

'It's our last chance to get a goal,' said Karen.

'But it isn't going to happen,' said Joe.

'What a pessimist●!' said Karen.

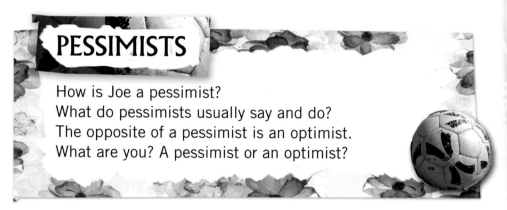

PESSIMISTS

How is Joe a pessimist?
What do pessimists usually say and do?
The opposite of a pessimist is an optimist.
What are you? A pessimist or an optimist?

Out on the pitch, Matt had control of the ball. He passed it to Gary. Gary manoeuvred● the ball up the field, but Rick was in his way●. Gary kicked the ball to Matt, and Matt passed the ball back to Gary. Gary shot● across the field.

'Look at him!' said Laura. 'How can he move so fast?'

'Because he's got big feet,' said Karen laughing.

Gary moved like lightning●. Everything happened in an instant. He kicked the ball. The ball flew● into the net. The goalkeeper was on the ground. The spectators● were shouting and screaming and jumping up and down.

Glossary

- **flew:** went quickly
- **in his way:** obstructing him
- **like lightning:** very fast
- **manoeuvred:** moved
- **pessimist:** person with negative opinions
- **rolled his eyes:** showed he was annoyed
- **shot:** ran quickly
- **spectators:** people who watch sports

14

'Goal!' screamed Joe and Karen together.

'I can't believe it,' said Karen.

'One-nil,' shouted Joe. 'He did it. Gary did it!'

'Did we win?' said Laura who had no idea what was going on.

'Did we win?' said Joe. 'Where have you been, Laura? Yes, of course we won! We just beat• Manning High – the best junior team in the league•!'

In the distance they could hear someone chanting, 'I got the goal! I got the goal!' It was Gary. He was running in circles, waving• his arms above his head.

• **beat:** defeated
• **league:** group of teams

• **waving:** moving from side to side

'Look at him,' said Karen in disgust●. 'He's mad!
Joe and the girls waited for Gary and Matt by the main gates. When the two boys arrived, they were smiling all over their faces.

'I got the goal,' said Gary. 'I hope you all saw that!'

'Only one goal,' said Karen, 'and you were lucky. You missed some good opportunities●.'

'No, I didn't,' said Gary.

'I was watching,' said Karen, 'I saw the shots you missed●.'
Gary went very red in the face. 'You think you're so smart●!' he said. 'You think you know everything about football and you know nothing.'

'Your problem, Gary,' said Karen, 'is that you think you know everything about the game, but you don't. In fact...' Karen stepped forward and prodded● Gary in the chest with her finger. 'In fact, Gary, you think that you know everything about everything, but you don't.'

'Oh yes?' said Gary. He pushed Karen's hand away and moved forward. Matt and Joe watched the scene, uncertain about what to do.

'Oh yes!' said Karen.

'Stop it!' said Laura. 'No more arguing. I don't know what's wrong with the two of you. You should be celebrating, not fighting.'

'She started it,' said Gary.

'That's quite enough,' said Laura. 'We're all going for a pizza and I don't want to hear another word from either of you!'

ARGUMENTS

Have you ever had an argument with anyone, or have you ever seen two people arguing?

What was the argument about? How did you feel during the argument?

Who won the argument? Did anyone help to end the disagreement?

Glossary

- **in disgust:** showing she does not approve
- **missed:** (here) didn't get a goal
- **opportunities:** chances
- **prodded:** pushed
- **smart:** clever; intelligent

FOOTBALL AMBITIONS

Gary arrived home later that afternoon. The argument with Karen was still annoying him, but he tried to forget it. The house was in darkness and it was chilly° inside the hallway. These days the house was often empty when he got home. He went into the kitchen, put on the lights and switched on the radio. Then he looked inside the fridge and took out a can of fizzy° orange. He looked in the biscuit tin° but it was empty.

He felt something brush against his legs. A large ginger° and white cat was looking up at him and purring°.

'Hi, Mr Brownie, I suppose you want your dinner?'

The cat miaowed. Gary opened a small tin of cat food and dumped° it into a saucer on the kitchen floor. Then he went in search of a packet of crisps.

HOME ALONE

Why is Gary's house empty?

How does Gary feel about being alone in the house?

Do you like being on your own in your own home?

What do you do at home when you are alone?

Glossary

- **ambitions:** hopes and plans for the future
- **chilly:** cold
- **dumped:** threw; put
- **fizzy:** with bubbles (like lemonade)
- **ginger:** orange
- **purring:** making cat sounds
- **tin:** container for food

18

In the lounge° Gary threw himself onto the sofa and switched on the TV. He flicked° through the channels and found some cartoons. As he relaxed among the cushions and ate his crisps, he found himself studying the photographs on the walls. There was a framed black and white newspaper photo of dad kicking a football. Next to that there was a colour photo of his dad receiving a football trophy°. Then, on the sideboard°, there was a large framed photo of the whole football team. His dad was in the front row°. Gary took a sip° of orange from the can. He was going to be a professional° footballer like his dad. And this was going to be his lucky year. First he was going to join the Crossbridge Football Academy. Then they would select him for the National Skills Final, and that meant he would get into the Under 17s team. After that he would soon be star – a football star like his dad. There was no doubt about it. His success was guaranteed°.

- **flicked:** changed channels quickly using the remote control
- **guaranteed:** sure
- **lounge:** (here) living room
- **professional:** paid to play football
- **row:** line
- **sideboard:** piece of furniture
- **sip:** small drink
- **trophy:** prize; award

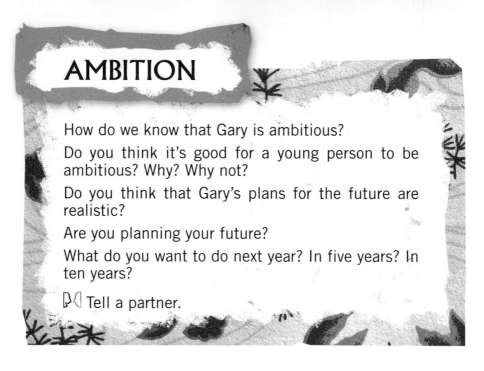

AMBITION

How do we know that Gary is ambitious?

Do you think it's good for a young person to be ambitious? Why? Why not?

Do you think that Gary's plans for the future are realistic?

Are you planning your future?

What do you want to do next year? In five years? In ten years?

Tell a partner.

Gary was just fifteen, but he already knew what he wanted to do. Life wasn't easy since his dad's company closed. His parents were much more careful about money now. They always said to him: 'Switch off• the lights, Gary. Don't waste• food, Gary. Don't throw your money away, Gary.' Only his mother had a job – in a dry -cleaning shop. So, right now they had to be careful with money, but soon he would have all the money he could dream of.

A door slammed•.

'Anyone home?' shouted a voice.

'Me,' said Gary.

A tall dark-haired man appeared in the doorway of the lounge.

'So, how was the match?' asked the man.

Glossary

- **slammed:** banged; closed with a loud noise
- **switch off:** turn off
- **waste:** use more than you need

'Hi, Dad! I scored a goal – the only goal.'

'Brilliant*,' said his dad. 'I knew you could do it. I'm really sorry I couldn't come. I had that interview today.'

'How did it go?'

'Oh, they'll call me if they need someone.' Gary saw that his dad was disappointed.

'That's tough,' said Gary.

'Don't worry,' said his dad, 'when you're a professional footballer you can help your poor old dad. I won't need to look for jobs then.' He turned around and went into the kitchen.

Gary continued looking at the photos on the walls. There was one of him when he was a baby. That was around the time when his dad hurt his knee playing in a game. Today doctors can fix* knee problems, but when his dad was a footballer, they couldn't do anything to help him. He had to leave the team. His life changed completely after that. It took him a long time to find work, but eventually* he got a job as the Marketing Manager of a sportswear* company. Then about a year ago the company closed down. Now he was always on his way to a job interview, or just coming back from one. Gary decided that would never happen to him. He gave his knees a little tap*.They were fine. 'Good,' thought Gary.

Glossary

- **brilliant:** very good
- **eventually:** after a period of time
- **fix:** mend; make better
- **sportswear:** clothes we wear for sports activities
- **tap:** knock; light hit

DANGEROUS SPORTS

Study this list of popular sporting activities.
Write the names of the sports under the pictures.

🗩 Work with a partner and decide which is the safest sport
and which is the most dangerous. Number them from 1 to 8

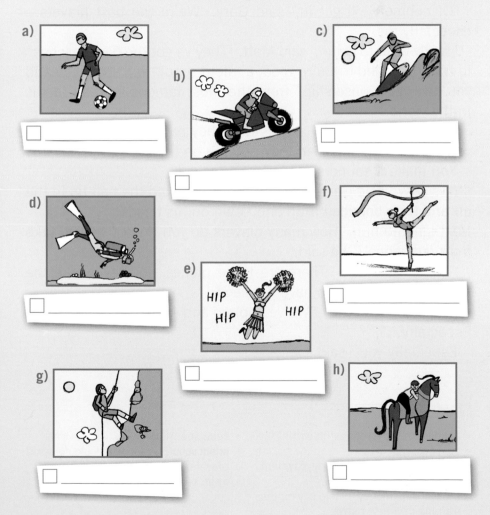

a)

b)

c)

d)

e)

f)

g)

h)

THE BEST

Gary, Matt and Joe were walking through the park on their way to school. Gary was kicking a ball through the grass.

'What do you think?' said Joe. 'Will we get into the Football Academy?'

'They say it's difficult,' said Matt.

'Of course we'll get in,' said Gary. 'We're the best players – especially me.'

'I really want to get in,' said Matt. 'They've got the best coaches• to train• you and if you're good, a talent scout• will spot• you and you can get sponsorship• from the most famous football teams in the world.'

'The best part,' said Gary, 'is that they pay you a salary• while you are training and then they put you on their team.'

'You make it sound so easy,' said Joe.

'It is easy,' said Gary. 'Look at me.' He kicked the ball up in the air and then bounced it up and down on his head.

Matt ignored him. 'How many players do you think they will take from our school?' he said.

'Three,' said Joe. 'There are three places, so they'll take the three best players who have applied•.'

'That's us,' said Gary. 'We've applied and we're the best players. Especially...'

'Especially you,' said Joe.

Glossary

- **applied:** made a request in writing
- **coaches:** teachers
- **salary:** a monthly or yearly payment for your work
- **sponsorship:** money to help pay for the training of a new player
- **spot:** see; notice
- **talent scout:** person who looks for good players
- **train:** teach (usually a sport)

'Right,' said Matt, 'but actually four people have applied.'
'Four?' said Gary.
'Yes, four,' said Joe. 'Karen has applied too.'
'Karen?' said Gary, dropping the ball, 'but she's a girl. They'll never take a girl.'

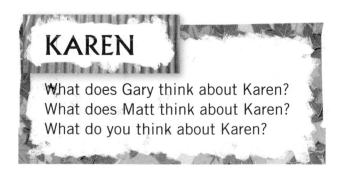

KAREN

What does Gary think about Karen?
What does Matt think about Karen?
What do you think about Karen?

'Well, then we don't have anything to worry about,' said Matt.

There was a dark blue BMW outside the main entrance of the school that morning. In the back window there was a sticker. It said 'Crossbridge Football Academy – the best training for the best players.' Karen was peering inside the car.

'This is Mr Page's car,' said Karen. 'I can see Rick's old green jumper on the back seat.'

'I bet Mr Page is really angry that Rick lost the match,' said Matt.

'He should come to me for lessons!' said Gary.

'Yes,' said Karen. 'You can be Mr Football, head coach of Mr Gary Football's Football Academy!'

OFFICE

Glossary

- **peering:** looking
- **sticker:** small piece of paper with writing etc. that you can stick/fix on something else

The first lesson that morning was Maths. Just as they went into the classroom, Mrs Morada, the headmaster's assistant, came to get them.

'Matt, Joseph, Gary and Karen,' said Mrs Morada, 'can you please come to Mr Steele's office during the morning break? 11 o'clock. Don't be late.'

'They're going to tell us who they've chosen,' Joe whispered to the others.

At 11 o'clock Matt, Joe and Karen were sitting outside Mr Steele's office. Gary arrived late.

'It's five past eleven,' said Karen.

Gary gave her an irritated° look.

Matt looked worried. 'I wonder° who they'll choose?'

'Well,' said Gary, 'They'll choose me... and then they'll choose me, and...'

Matt and Joe started to laugh.

'What about Karen?' said Joe, 'Will they choose her?'

'They've already chosen her, but she isn't going to the Football Academy. She's going to Manchester United. She's going to be their new tea lady°!'

'Very funny,' said Karen.

The door to Mr Steele's office opened.

'Good morning, boys,' he said.

Karen stared at him.

'And Karen,' he said. 'Come in. Come in.'

Matt, Joe, Gary and Karen filed° into his room.

THOUGHTS

We don't always say what we think. Whose thoughts are these?

a) 'Why doesn't she mind her own business?'
b) 'I don't think that's very funny.'
c) 'Don't forget that I'm here too, and I'm a girl.'
d) 'Oh! I made a mistake. Karen's angry with me.'

Glossary

- **filed:** walked in one by one
- **irritated:** annoyed; a little angry
- **tea lady:** woman whose job is to make and serve tea
- **wonder:** ask yourself

THE SELECTION

Inside the office, a man with a suntanned face and very short silver-grey hair sat in a chair next to Mr Steele's desk.

'This is Brian Page. I think you know him. He's Rick's father and, of course, he is the Senior Coach at the Crossbridge Football Academy. He's also Head of Admissions, and that's why he is here today to talk to you.'

'Yes, thank you, Mr Steele, and good morning to all of you,' said Mr Page. 'As you know, this year we have three free places at the Academy for students from Crossbridge School. The selected students will attend coaching sessions° four times a week after school and on alternate Saturdays°. We need serious commitment° from our students. This means they have to come on time to the coaching sessions, they have to attend regularly, and they have to get a C-grade average – or above – in their schoolwork. We want all our students to have a good academic record°. They should have brains as well as physical ability.'

1ST PRIZE
Crossbridge High
Winner
Man of the Match
Gary Cummings

- **academic record:** school grades
- **alternate Saturdays:** once every two Saturdays
- **commitment:** promise to do something
- **sessions:** periods of time for activities, etc.

Matt and Joe shifted° restlessly° from foot to foot. Karen bit her nails. Gary studied the football trophies next to him in the display cabinet° by the wall. 'So,' continued Mr Page, 'when we read your applications, in addition to football skills, we looked for evidence of punctuality, good attendance, and high marks in school subjects. We could only choose three of you so I'm sorry that one of you will be disappointed°.'

All eyes were now on Mr Page. 'We would like to offer places on the Crossbridge Football Academy training scheme to Matt, Joseph and... Karen.' Matt and Joe gave gasps° of relief and slapped their hands together. Karen's face widened into a large smile. Gary stood immobile°. He had a puzzled° expression on his face.

WOW!

Glossary

- **disappointed:** sad and upset because you didn't get what you hoped for
- **display cabinet:** cupboard with glass for showing obects
- **gasps:** fast, short breaths of air
- **immobile:** not moving
- **puzzled:** confused
- **restlessly:** without peace; always moving
- **shifted:** moved
- **stunned:** shocked

'I'm sorry we weren't able to offer you a place, Gary,' said Mr Page. 'Maybe next time.'

Matt and Joe fell silent and looked at each other, and then at Gary. Gary did not look at them. He just stared ahead. He was stunned•. Thoughts flashed through his mind: 'Why did they choose the others and not me? What will I do now? What will dad say?' He felt like crying.

'Matt, Joseph and Karen,' said Mr Steele, 'congratulations to all of you. You can go back to class.'

Gary turned and walked towards the door.

'Gary, can you stay behind? I need to talk to you,' said Mr Steele.

DISAPPOINTMENT

Can you think of a time when you were as disappointed as Gary?

What happened to disappoint you?

What do you think Mr Steele is going to say to Gary?

31

LIKE FATHER, LIKE SON

'I'm sorry, Gary,' said Mr Steele. 'I know you're disappointed, but you have low marks● in both English and Maths. You know that.'
Gary stared● at his feet.
Mr Steele continued. 'The trainees● at the Football Academy have to do a lot of reading and writing as part of the course, and your schoolwork just isn't up to standard●.'

'David Beckham didn't need English or Maths,' said Gary.

'Actually, Gary,' said Mr Steele, 'David Beckham's best subject at school was Maths. He's a footballer and he's also a businessman. Footballers can't be footballers for ever. Don't be upset●. You'll have another chance to go to the Academy next year.'

'But next year's too late,' Gary protested●, 'I'm already fifteen. I'll be too old when I'm sixteen.'

'Nonsense●,' said Mr Steele. 'I want you to go away, work hard and improve your schoolwork. You'll see that everything will work out●.'
When Gary stepped into the corridor, Matt was waiting for him.

'Gary, I'm really sorry,' said Matt. 'You deserved● that place at the Academy, not me.'

'It doesn't matter,' said Gary, but they both knew that it did matter. It mattered very much indeed.

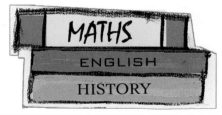

Glossary

- **deserved:** you should have got it
- **marks:** grades in school
- **nonsense:** that's not true
- **protested:** complained; disagreed
- **stared:** looked without moving his eyes
- **trainees:** students
- **up to standard:** of good quality
- **upset:** angry and sad
- **work out:** be solved

'I don't understand,' said Gary's father. 'You were so sure about getting in. What went wrong? Who did they take?'

'Matt and Joe,' said Gary.

'I thought they took three,' said his dad, 'Who was the third player?'

'Karen,' he said. 'They gave the other place to Karen.'

Gary's dad sat down on the sofa, sighed● and shook his head. He took a sip of tea from his mug. 'Your mum's going to be very upset,' he said. 'You'd better stay out of the way. I'll tell her when she comes home.'

Gary went upstairs to his room. He lay on the bed and stared up at the ceiling●. The walls of the room were covered with pennants of all the famous international clubs and posters of his favourite players. Gary wanted to be like them. He wanted to be one of them. But he was just a stupid kid who was crazy about football and had footballers' pictures on his walls.

In the distance he heard voices. Maybe his mum was home. He felt bad. He heard footsteps. Someone knocked on the door. The door opened.

'Gary?'

Glossary

- **bothering:** causing problems for
- **ceiling:** roof in a room
- **railings:** fence made of metal
- **sighed:** took a deep breath of air, expressing tiredness
- **warehouses:** buildings where people store things

It was Matt.

'Matt, what are you doing here?' said Gary.

'We came to get you – me, Joe and Karen. Come and play some football with us. Joe and Karen are waiting downstairs. We're still your friends, aren't we?'

It was true. Everything was just the same. They walked until they reached a street with railings● on one side and warehouses● on the other two sides. No one came here after half past five. They could play without bothering● anyone. Joe agreed to be goalkeeper. It took Gary three or four tries, but then the ball shot past Matt and Karen. Joe tried to catch the ball but he missed it.

'Goal!' shouted Gary as the ball bounced off the door of the warehouse.

The ball hit the ground, rolled onto the pavement and stopped in front of a pair of white trainers. A tall blond boy wearing a blue tracksuit picked it up.

'Rick,' said Gary, 'What are you doing here?'

'I came to watch your last game,' said Rick smiling.

'What do you mean?' said Gary.

'After today your friends are going to be busy at the Academy. They won't have any more time to play football with you. You'll have to play with the kids from the primary school.' He laughed.

'Leave us alone, Rick,' said Karen, 'Come on, Gary. Let's go home.'

'No, I'm afraid I can't leave you alone, Karen,' said Rick. 'I'm going to be at the Academy too. You're going to see me four evenings a week and every other Saturday, too.'

Glossary

- **pavement:** footpath
- **rolled:** moved along the ground
- **trainers:** sports shoes

36

A car horn sounded. Rick kicked the ball into the air. Then he strolled●, still smiling, towards the blue BMW that was waiting at the end of the street. Before he reached the car he turned around and shouted, 'Hey, Gary, how do you feel? They chose a girl instead of you!' The car drove away. Gary and the others didn't feel like playing any more after that.

'That boy Gary,' said Mr Page as he and Rick drove home, 'he's going to be just like his father. Useless●.'

'His dad was a footballer, wasn't he?' said Rick. 'I thought he had to stop because he had an injury●.'

'Who knows?' said Mr Page. 'They say he had a knee injury. He was probably just a bad player and they threw him out of the team. Gary will be the same. His father can't find a job and he can't get into the Academy. You know the saying, "Like father, like son".'

● **injury:** physical damage
● **strolled:** walked slowly
● **useless:** not good at anything

Rick was silent, then he said, 'Dad, can I have a new MP3 player?'

'Of course you can,' said Mr Page. 'You deserve it. You passed your English and Maths tests and you got into the Academy. You can have anything you want. I'm proud of you.'

RICK

Which of the following words describe Rick? Give reasons for your choice.

- ☐ kind
- ☐ thoughtful
- ☐ cruel
- ☐ friendly
- ☐ jealous
- ☐ greedy
- ☐ quiet
- ☐ generous

Can you think of any other words or expressions that describe Rick?

In what way is Rick similar to or different from his father?

DAD, CAN I HAVE...

NO PROBLEM

It was Saturday. Normally Gary went to the park on Saturday morning to play football with Matt, Joe and Karen. Today they were at the Academy, and they were going to be there all day. Gary was missing* them already. Sprawled* on his bed next to Mr Brownie, he studied the Crossbridge Football Academy application form. There would be another opportunity to take the entry test in six weeks. There were no more free places, but he could get in if he passed the test and paid the fees*.

> **Glossary**
>
> • **fees:** cost of a school or course
> • **missing:** when you are sad that someone is not with you
> • **sprawled:** lying in a relaxed way

He took the form downstairs. In the kitchen his father was making some tea and his mother was reading the newspaper.

'You look very serious this morning, Gary,' said his mum.

'I was thinking about how to get into the Academy,' said Gary.

'But it's too late now, isn't it?' said his dad.

'I can take the test again in six weeks, but if I pass, I'll have to pay. It says so on this application form,' said Gary.

'Let me have a look,' said Dad. His dad examined the form. He frowned● when he looked at the list of fees.

'What do you think?' he said passing the form to Gary's mum. She frowned too when she saw the cost.

'Sorry, son,' said Gary's dad, 'we just can't afford● it.'

'Well,' said his mum, 'we can afford to pay some of the cost, but not all of it. We could pay half. You could pay the other half. You could get a job – a paper round● or something like that, but what about the test? Do you think you can pass it?'

Gary thought for a moment. 'No problem, mum,' he said. 'I'll pass the test and I'll get a job. You'll see!'

PROMISES

What does Gary promise his parents?

Do you think he can keep his promise? Why? Why not?

Have you ever made an important promise to your parents or to a close friend?

Did you keep your promise or break your promise?

Glossary

- **afford:** have enough money for
- **frowned:** made an expression of unhappiness

- **paper round:** job delivering newspapers to people's houses

In his room, Gary opened his Maths book and stared at the page in front of him. He closed his Maths book and opened his English book. He read a few pages, then he closed his book. He sighed. He had no idea how he could pass that test.

Crossbridge Football Academy was a large modern building, built on the edge of town. It had every facility° that you could imagine. There was a huge° football field, a swimming pool, a shop selling sports equipment, classrooms, a gym, even a small cinema, and a cafeteria. Matt, Joe and Karen found the cafeteria immediately and sat there at the end of their first day at the Academy. The cafeteria was full of young people laughing and chattering°.

'I think they're enjoying themselves,' said Matt.

'Well, I didn't enjoy myself,' said Joe.

'No, neither did I,' said Matt. 'Something's missing.'

'Gary's missing,' said Joe.

'It's not the same without him,' said Karen.

'Oh, you poor children,' said a voice. Rick was standing by their table with a sports bag in one hand. 'You're all alone and your little friend is far away,' he said. 'Well, get used to it°. Gary isn't coming here. He just isn't good enough.' Rick threw his bag over his shoulder and walked away.

'I'm not enjoying myself and I don't like it here,' said Joe.

'We need to do something about Gary,' said Karen.

'I've got a plan,' said Matt.

Glossary

- **chattering:** talking quickly about unimportant things
- **facility:** place to do activities
- **get used to it:** accept it
- **huge:** very big

42

A PLAN FOR GARY

Gary looked worried. He was in Matt's house, sitting at the dining-room table. Matt, Joe and Karen sat opposite him. They were very serious. They did not smile.

'We're going to help you, Gary,' said Matt.

'I don't need any help,' said Gary.

'Believe us, Gary. You need help,' said Joe.

'Do you know Laura?' said Karen.

'Yes, of course I know Laura,' said Gary. 'She's Matt's sister.'

'Well, she's going to be your teacher,' said Karen.

'What do you mean?' Gary started to panic.

'She's training to be a teacher,' said Matt. 'She's going to help you with your Maths and English.'

'You mean she's going to experiment• on me?' said Gary.

'She's a very good teacher,' said Matt. 'She's agreed to teach you so that you can pass the Academy test.'

Gary sat back in his chair. 'Oh!' he said.

'OK,' Gary said. 'So, I take the test, I pass it and I get into the Academy. How am I going to pay the fees?'

'We've thought of that,' said Joe.

'Yes, we've thought of everything,' said Karen. 'We've found you a job.'

Gary sighed.

Glossary

• **experiment:** try new ideas

HELPING PEOPLE

Have you ever helped someone?
What did you do and why did you do it?

In pairs or groups write the dialogue of the situation then act it out.

How are Matt, Joe and Karen going to help Gary?

How do you think Gary feels about their plan to help him?

When is it not a good idea to help someone?

Give an example.

Gary felt very miserable● indeed when he walked home that afternoon. Now he had to study, and he had to go to work. But why? He only wanted to be a footballer.

The last person Gary wanted to see that afternoon was Rick. Carl and Jeff were with him. Gary didn't like them either. Gary noticed they were all wearing new football shirts and trainers. Their parents had plenty of money.

'Hey, Gary!' shouted Rick. 'What's two and two? Or do you need a calculator?'

The boys pushed past Gary and walked down the street laughing at him. Everyone at school knew about the Academy and they knew that Gary had failed his Maths and English tests. Maybe he did need help after all.

Glossary

● **miserable:** sad; unhappy

TROUBLE AT THE FISH AND CHIP SHOP

Gary needed a job, but he didn't need *this* job. It was awful. His hair was full of grease° and his clothes smelt of fish.

'I'd like three portions° of fish and chips, please,' said Joe. He stood with Matt at the front of a long queue° of customers.

'And can I have extra chips, please,' said Matt. 'Remember. I'm your friend.'

'Karen wants ketchup on her chips,' said Joe.

'Yes, hurry up! We're hungry,' shouted Karen from the back of the shop. She didn't want the smell of fish on her clothes.

Gary was standing behind the counter of Reji Kumar's fish and chip shop. He was wearing a white T-shirt and a little white cap. Behind him, in the kitchen, Jason the cook busily fried pieces of fish and mountains of chips. Jason did the cooking. Gary served the customers. He put packets of hot fish and chips into yellow paper bags.

'You forgot the chips,' said Matt, looking inside his paper bag. Gary picked up three small packets of chips and stuffed° them into Matt's yellow bag.

'There,' he said. 'Pay at the cash desk, please.' He pointed to the door where Mrs Kumar sat in front of a cash register°, reading her newspaper.

- **cash register:** machine that makes calculations and holds money
- **grease:** oil
- **portions:** quantities for one person
- **queue:** line of people waiting
- **stuffed:** put quickly and with force

PART-TIME JOBS

Are children and young people allowed to work in your country?
How old must they be?
Have you ever had a part-time job? What was it like?

'You look very silly° in that hat,' said Karen, who had come to the front of the queue to get her fish.

'Please. I'm working,' said Gary.

'Don't push in,' said a large man with a red face who was standing behind Matt.

Glossary

- **cod:** a type of fish
- **pale:** with white skin
- **plaice:** a type of fish
- **silly:** stupid

'I'm not pushing in,' said Karen. 'My friends were here first.'

'Can you hurry up!' said a pale• young man standing behind the man with the red face.

'Yes, how long do we have to wait in this queue?' said an old woman who was standing behind him.

'Excuse me,' said a boy in a green T-shirt, 'I wanted plaice• and chips, but you gave me cod• and chips.'

'Isn't that plaice?' said Gary. 'I thought it was plaice.'

'Hey, these chips are cold,' said a girl in a black leather jacket and jeans. She waved a half-eaten bag of chips in Gary's face.

'That's not my fault,' said Gary. 'You ate them too slowly.'

'I want my money back!' said the girl.

The noise in the shop was rising. Mrs Kumar looked up from her newspaper. Matt, Joe and Karen paid at the cash desk. Then, as they left the shop, Rick and Carl walked in.

By this time everyone was complaining. Rick pushed through the crowd of customers and went up to the counter.

'Hello, Gary,' he said in a loud voice. 'I have a question for you. If I have ten chips and I eat five, how many do I have left? Two? Three?'

Rick and Carl burst into laughter•.

'Listen, everybody,' said Rick. 'Make sure you check your chips. Mr Football here can't count.'

Gary threw off his white cap and came out from behind the counter•. From the kitchen, Jason shouted, 'That's not a good idea, Gary!'

Mrs Kumar called her husband on his mobile phone. 'Reji!' she said, 'Come to the shop now. There's trouble!'

TROUBLE

What do you think Gary is going to do?
What do you think Reji Kumar is going to say?
What would you do in Gary's situation?

▷◁ In groups of 3 write the conversation between Reji Kumar, Gary and Rick.
Act it out in class.

Glossary

- **burst into laughter:** started laughing suddenly and loudly
- **counter:** high desk in a shop (see illustration)

'All right, that's enough!' said Reji Kumar. 'It's time for you to go. Get your things and I'll give you your money.'

'I didn't do anything,' said Gary.

'I don't want troublemakers• working in my shop,' said Mr Kumar.

'It was Rick Page. He started it,' said Gary.

'I know Brian Page. His son is not a troublemaker, but you are. When you learn to behave more responsibly, you can come back and work in my shop.'

'Sorry,' said Gary.

'I gave you this job as a favour, Gary. Joseph is my nephew• and he said you were a hard worker. He didn't say that you would get into arguments with my customers and start fights.'

'Sorry,' said Gary.

'Thank you for your help, Gary, and goodbye,' said Mr Kumar.

The next time that Matt, Joe and Karen saw Rick at the Academy, he had a black eye.

'Oh dear,' said Joe, 'Did you fall over your football? You must be more careful.'

Rick's face turned red.

'You mind your own business•, Joseph Kumar,' he said. 'Your little friend Gary isn't going to pass the entry test and he isn't going to come to the Academy. No one will give him a job and he hasn't got any money.'

'Sorry I spoke' said Joe.

GARY'S NEW JOB

The Gary problem had just got worse. Matt, Joe and Karen held a meeting in the park. They sat around Gary in a semicircle on the grass.

'Now I'm in big trouble,' said Joe. 'My uncle isn't speaking to me. Why did you start a fight? That job was such a good opportunity.'

'Yes, and you got free fish and chips,' said Karen.

'I don't like fish and chips,' said Gary. 'And Rick started the fight, not me.'

'Go back next week and say you're sorry,' said Joe. 'I'll try to speak to my uncle. He's angry now but next week he'll be better. I'm sure he'll give you your job back.'

'What do you think?' said Matt.

'No,' said Gary. 'I'm not going back.'

There was silence.

'Well,' said Karen after a long pause, 'they need some part-timers° at the supermarket where I work. Maybe I can get you a job there.'

Gary stood up, ran across the grass and then kicked his football up into the air.

'He only thinks about football,' said Matt.

'We can't help him if he won't help himself,' said Joe.

Gary met Karen outside the staff° entrance of the Pricewise supermarket. A burly° security guard° called Ray unlocked the door and let them in.

'Morning, Ray,' said Karen. 'This is Gary.'

'Nice to meet you, Gary,' said Ray, shaking Gary's hand.

'He's really excited about coming to work with us, aren't you, Gary?' Gary gave Karen a murderous look°. The last thing he wanted was to give up° his Sunday mornings, but he had no choice.

It was 7:45 am. He put on his red and white Pricewise T-shirt and followed Karen into the main part of the shop.

OPENING HOURS

What are the opening hours for shops in your country?
Do you think supermarkets should stay open 7 days a week?
Do you think supermarkets should open 24 hours a day?

'Now, listen carefully,' she said. 'This is the furniture polish[•] and you must put it here in the Cleaning Materials section. Do you understand?'

'Yes, I know. I can do that. It's easy.'

'No, you don't know,' said Karen. 'I'm showing you how to do it now.'

'All right. All right,' said Gary.

'All the tubes in these boxes should go in the Personal Hygiene[•] section. Got that?'

'Yes, Karen, I'm not stupid. I can do that,' said Gary.

'Fine,' said Karen, 'Call me if you need me. I'll be in Breakfast Cereals.'

Glossary

- **hygiene:** staying healthy and clean
- **polish:** cream to make furniture clean and shiny

An hour later, Mr Moore the manager checked the shelves.

'Karen,' he said. 'Are you teaching the new boy to fill the shelves?' He looked puzzled.

'Yes,' Mr Moore,' said Karen. 'Is anything wrong?'

'He's put the furniture polish on the same shelf as the toothpaste, and he's put the washing-up liquid in the same section as the shampoo.'

Karen smiled. 'No problem, Mr Moore. I'll talk to him. He just needs a few more lessons.'

'I can't believe you did that,' said Karen. She and Gary were on their way home. 'How could you mix everything up like that?'

'It's a stupid job,' said Gary.

'Maybe it is stupid,' said Karen, 'but remember why you're doing it.'

Gary said nothing. When they reached his house, he went into the garden and picked up his football.

'What are you doing?' said Karen.

'I'm going to play football in the park,' said Gary.

'No you're not,' said Karen. 'You've got a lesson with Laura now. Have you forgotten? She's waiting for you.'

Gary gave a sigh, then threw down the football.

'Go and get your books. I'll wait for you,' said Karen.

Gary went into the house. Karen waited outside for fifteen minutes. There was no sign of Gary. She went into the house to hurry him up. She heard voices. Someone was watching television. She walked into the lounge. Gary was relaxing on the sofa, eating a bag of crisps.

'Gary,' she said in a very loud voice. 'Go to your lesson now. Do you hear me? Go now!'

ANSWER THE QUESTIONS

Why isn't Joe's uncle speaking to him?

Why does Gary need more lessons to work in the supermarket?

How does Gary try to avoid his lesson with Laura?

People sometimes try to avoid doing things they don't like. Can you think of some examples?

58

Fruit and Vegetables

LABELS

On the next two Sunday mornings, Gary was late for his job. It was easy for him to get up early and play football. It was very difficult for him to get up early and go to work. Mr Moore checked the shelves regularly because Gary usually put things in the wrong places. On the third Sunday, Mr Moore heard the sound of a can rolling along the floor. He turned a corner and saw Gary jumping from side to side as he dribbled° a can of tuna along the ground.

Glossary

- **dribbled:** ran while kicking the ball lightly

When he reached the Cleaning Materials section, he gave the can a sharp kick. It flew along the ground and crashed into the washing powder display. Gary punched his fist in the air and shouted:

'Goal!'

When he turned, Mr Moore stood in front of him with his arms folded.

'Can I remind you, Gary, that this is a supermarket, not a football field?'

'Sorry, Mr Moore,' said Gary and he quickly put the boxes of washing powder back in place. He picked up the can of tuna and carried it back to its place.

'Hello, Gary,' said Rick, 'I've come to make a complaint•.'

'Go away,' said Gary, 'I'm busy.'

'Oh, he's busy,' Rick said to Carl and Jeff.

'You're going to be even busier,' he said to Gary.

Gary frowned. 'What do you mean,' he said.

'Well, all your labels are wrong,' said Rick.

Gary looked around. The label under the peas said 'Mushrooms,' the label under the tinned meat said 'Soup,' the label on the tinned fish shelf said 'Fresh Eggs.'

'Oh no!' said Gary.

The three boys burst into laughter. Before leaving the supermarket they bought some chocolate bars from a display labelled 'Carrots.'

Glossary
_____

• **make a complaint:** report something that is wrong or that you are unhappy about

PRACTICAL JOKES

Rick and his friends play a practical joke on Gary.
Has anyone ever played a joke like this on you?
Or did you play a joke on someone else?

Tell the class what happened.

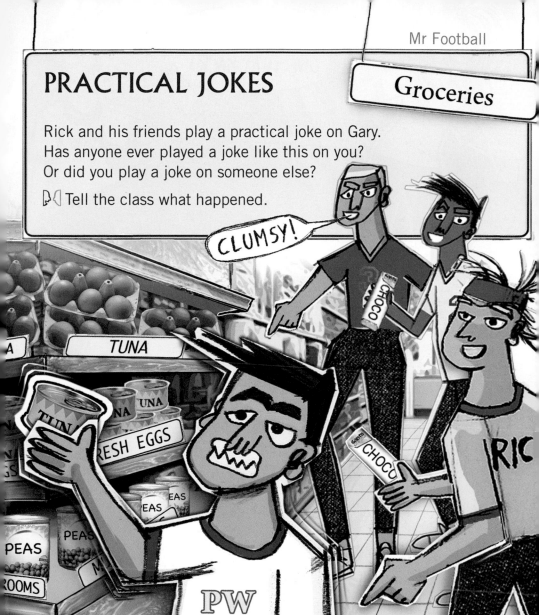

'Mr Moore is not happy with you,' said Karen.
As she and Gary walked home.

'Well, I'm not happy with Mr Moore,' said Gary.

'He spoils● my football practice.'

'Gary, have you forgotten why you are doing that job?' said Karen. Gary said nothing.

'You're earning● money so that you can go to the Football Academy.

Gary bounced his football in the direction of the park. Karen ran in front of him.

'You've got a lesson with Laura, Gary!'
Gary didn't look at her. Karen grabbed the football.

'Hey! Give that back,' shouted Gary, but Karen was already kicking the ball along the road in the direction of Laura's house.

'That's not fair,' said Gary, 'That was a foul●!'

Glossary

● **a foul:** against the rules
● **earning:** getting money for work

● **spoils:** ruins

PEAS

Gary tried his best*. He worked harder than he had ever worked. He put the right things on the right shelves. He checked the labels on the shelves. He built impressive* food displays*. He stayed calm when Rick came to the supermarket... even when Rick called him names.

'Just ignore him,' said Karen. 'He'll go away.'

But Rick didn't go away. On Gary's fourth Sunday at the Pricewise supermarket, something bad happened.

Gary built a very tall display of peas. It looked like a tower. Gary had to stand on a ladder to put the last cans on the top of the tower. That's when he saw Rick.

GUESS

What happens next?
Write the next part of the story with a partner

- **displays:** objects for the public to see and admire
- **impressive:** amazing; incredible
- **tried his best:** did things as well as possible

63

ADVICE

What advice does Karen give Gary about Rick?
What advice would you give Gary?
Has anyone ever given you advice?
Was it helpful or did it annoy you?

🗩 Tell the class about your experience.

'Hello, Gary,' he said, 'I just popped in° to buy a can of peas.' He leaned over to the fourth row° of the display and took hold of° the can in the middle. 'This one,' he said.

'Rick! Don't!' said Gary.

But it was too late.

Glossary

- **popped in:** came in for a quick visit
- **row:** horizontal line
- **took hold of:** took in his hand

Gary never wanted to see another can of peas again. But soon he forgot about his horrible day at the supermarket. He dribbled his football along the pavement. At last he was free and he was going to play street football with Matt and Joe. When he arrived, he realized something was wrong. Matt and Joe were sitting by the railings. They looked miserable. Karen was with them.

'Hello,' said Gary, 'Who's going to be goalkeeper first?'

'Gary, we know,' said Matt.

'I don't know what you're talking about,' said Gary.

'You lost your job,' said Joe. 'We found you a good job and you lost it.'

'No, I didn't,' said Gary.

Joe looked at Karen.

'Mr Moore's exact words,' said Karen, 'were: "You will not destroy my shop, Gary. You will not fight in my shop. You will not upset the customers in my shop. And you will not work in my shop. Next Sunday is your last Sunday." That was what he said. I know. I was there.'

'In other words,' said Matt, 'you lost your job.'

'It wasn't my fault,' said Gary. 'It was Rick. He started it. He started a fight.'

Matt, Joe and Karen stared at Gary.

'Oh, all right. I lost my job. So what●?'

'So… we can't do anything else to help you,' said Matt.

'Sorry,' said Karen. 'We tried everything.'

'See you at school tomorrow,' said Joe.

● **so what?:** It doesn't matter.

Karen and the two boys left Gary standing there in the street. He watched them walk away down the road, then he kicked his football hard into the side of the warehouse.

Outside the Football Academy there was a large noticeboard. Gary stopped to have a look. There were photographs on the board of all the successful young players from the Academy. Now they were playing for top clubs all around the world. Gary stared at the faces of the lucky teenagers. They were just like him. He was just like them. He wanted his photograph to be next to theirs.

'Your picture won't ever be up there,' said a voice.
Gary started to walk away. That voice only meant trouble.

'I didn't know you could read,' said Rick.

'Leave me alone,' said Gary.

'They call you Mr Football,' said Rick, following him. 'But they should really call you Missed-A-Football•. You're going nowhere. You can't even do a stupid job in a supermarket. Face it•. You're a loser•.'

Gary wanted to turn around and hit him, but this time he just kept walking.

66

THE LOSER TAKES A CHANCE

Gary sat alone on a bench in the park. Some children were playing football on the grass. A small ginger-haired° boy ran over to him.

'Come and play with us, Mr Football,' he said.

'Not today, Terry. Maybe tomorrow.'

'OK,' said the boy, and he ran back to join the game.

Gary thought how it all seemed to be so easy. He was a fool°. He thought it was going to be easy, and that's why he never really made an effort°. He was a fool. Mr Steele was right. He needed more than ability to be a professional footballer. He needed to work hard and be committed°. Everyone had made an effort to help him, and he had let them down°. He shouldn't have been so sure of himself, and he shouldn't have been so lazy. Everything was a complete disaster – the jobs, his schoolwork, his friendships. Rick was right. He was a loser.

He looked at his watch. He was already twenty minutes late for his lesson with Laura. But then he thought, 'I'm already a loser. I've got nothing to lose. There's still a chance. There's always still a chance.' He stood up and walked across the park, then he started to run. He ran fast. He ran all the way to Laura and Matt's house.

Glossary

- **be committed:** do something in a serious and concentrated way
- **fool:** stupid person
- **ginger-haired:** with red hair
- **let them down:** caused them disappointment
- **made an effort:** worked hard

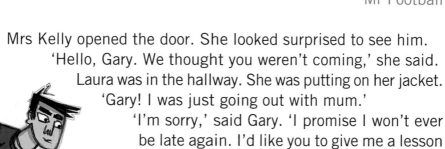

Mrs Kelly opened the door. She looked surprised to see him.
'Hello, Gary. We thought you weren't coming,' she said.
Laura was in the hallway. She was putting on her jacket.
'Gary! I was just going out with mum.'
'I'm sorry,' said Gary. 'I promise I won't ever
be late again. I'd like you to give me a lesson
… if it's not too much trouble. You see, I
really want to pass that test.'
Laura looked at her mother. She took
off her jacket.
'You go without me, Mum,' she said.
'Gary and I have got work to do.'

DECISIONS

What has Gary decided?
Why has he reached
this decision?

Have you – or perhaps
someone you know
– ever made any big
decisions?

Tell the class.

'I haven't seen Gary all week,' said Karen.

'I saw him yesterday in the Science lab,' said Joe. 'He was helping the teacher.'

'That's very strange,' said Karen. 'Do you think he's all right?'

'He's spending a lot of time with Laura,' said Matt.

'Do you think Gary fancies● your sister, Matt?' said Joe. 'Maybe he's in love.'

Matt hit Joe over the head with his exercise book.

'No, stupid, she's helping him prepare for the Academy entry test.'

Glossary

● **fancies:** likes in a romantic way

Gary sat at the dining-room table in Matt's house. He looked worried. Laura sat on the opposite side of the table. She was correcting Gary's Maths homework. She looked worried too. She looked at Gary.

'Well?' he said.

'It's brilliant,' she said. 'You're brilliant. You got everything right. I mean, just one small mistake.' She looked doubtful* for a moment. 'Did someone help you?'

'You did,' said Gary. 'I couldn't do it without you.'

Laura blushed*. 'I think you can pass this test, Gary. You've got a real talent.'

'For football,' said Gary.

'For Maths,' said Laura.

---

* **blushed:** went red because she was embarrassed

* **doubtful:** not sure

Gary crossed the park, bouncing his football in front of him.

'It's Mr Football! Come on, it's Mr Football!'

A group of six or seven children surrounded Gary. 'Please play with us, Mr Football,' said the smallest boy.

'No, I'm busy,' said Gary, 'I have to study for a test. It's very important.'

'You promised,' said Terry, the boy with the ginger hair.

Gary looked at his watch. 'OK,' he said. 'Just fifteen minutes, then I have to go.'

'Yes!' shouted the boys, and they ran around him in circles.

'Right,' said Gary, 'Let's get organized...'

Gary gave orders. He told the boys where to go and what to do. He got them to run around the flowerbeds* and then to do bending* and stretching* exercises.

'I'm tired,' protested one of the boys.

'After only ten minutes?' said Gary, 'You have to make an effort if you want to be a footballer. And,' he said, 'you have to be good at spelling and sums*.

The boys looked very disappointed. Then Terry said, 'He's Mr Football. He knows!'

Glossary

- **bending:** touching toes, etc.
- **flowerbeds:** area where flowers grow
- **squealing:** shouting in high voices
- **stretching:** extending arms and legs
- **sums:** Maths

The boys looked at each other, then one of them jumped in the air and shouted, 'Yes, we're good at spelling, sums and football, too!'

 'OK, I have to go now,' said Gary, 'but first you have to come and get your football.'

He ran as fast as he could to the park gate. The boys ran after him laughing and squealing• with excitement. At the gate he stopped, turned around and kicked the ball up high into the air. 'Remember,' he said, 'spelling and sums. See you tomorrow.'

IT'S A GOAL !

When Mr Moore arrived at the supermarket at 7:15 the following Sunday, he got the shock of his life. All the food displays were tidy and someone had swept° the floor of the storeroom°. He heard a noise in the Soft Drinks section. Someone was moving bottles about. He went to take a look and found Gary stacking° the shelves.

'Gary? It's 7:15. What are you doing here and how did you get in?'

'Sorry, Mr Moore. The security guard let me in. I hope that's alright.'

'Ray let you in? What time was that?' said Mr Moore.

'About a quarter to seven,' said Gary.

'Are you sure you're all right, Gary?' said Mr Moore.

'It's my last day,' said Gary, 'and I wanted to make sure I finished everything.'

'Oh,' said Mr Moore, 'I see. Well, come and see me around half past three and I'll give you your money.' Mr Moore walked back to his office, looking slightly confused.

Karen arrived just before eight o'clock.

'I didn't expect to see you here so early, Gary,' she said. 'Where were you this week? I've hardly seen you.'

'I've been studying,' said Gary.

'You're kidding°,' said Karen.

'No, really. The Academy entry test is at five o'clock today.'

'And you're going?' asked Karen.

'I'm going straight there after work.'

'I'm impressed,' said Karen.

Glossary

- **kidding:** joking; not serious
- **stacking:** putting things on shelves
- **storeroom:** room where you keep extra things
- **swept:** cleaned with a brush

74

Karen was even more impressed when she saw how efficiently Gary was working. He filled shelves, he checked prices, he threw away empty boxes, he swept up rubbish. He even helped customers to find what they wanted.

'You sit there, Mr Patel,' he said to an elderly gentleman. 'I'll get your bread for you.'

'Thank you, Gary. You're very kind,' said the old man.
A young woman with a screaming baby in a pram came to look for some baby food and disposable nappies.

'This way,' said Gary, and as the woman chose what she wanted, he bounced the baby up and down in his arms. He was quite enjoying himself.

'You're very good with babies,' said the woman. 'You can come and be my babysitter any time.'

'Thank you, but no thank you,' said Gary when he saw that it was time for a nappy change.

- **disposable:** that you can throw away
- **elderly gentleman:** old man
- **nappies:** underwear for babies
- **screaming:** crying loudly

75

A tall man with long greasy hair was wandering round the shop looking lost.

'Can I help you?' said Gary. The man looked surprised, maybe even a little nervous.

'Yes,' he said, 'Where are the men's deodorants and shaving° things?' Gary led him to some shelves at the back of the shop and wondered why the man was wearing a big overcoat when it was so warm outside.

At around twenty-five past three, when Gary was getting ready to go to Mr Moore's office, a shout came from the back of the shop. There was a loud crash, and then more shouting.

'What's going on?' said Karen.

'Watch out!' shouted Ray.

The man in the overcoat raced° out from behind the breakfast cereals and headed towards the exit.

'He's a shoplifter°,' shouted Ray.

The man ran like lightning past Gary. Gary made a quick decision. He ran at full speed° towards the display of peas. He took aim° and kicked. One can of peas shot along the ground and rolled under the man's feet. He lost his balance and he went sprawling° onto the floor.

'It's a goal!' shouted Gary. He couldn't stop himself. He punched his fist in the air and ran around in a circle with his arms waving in the air, jumping over the cans of peas that were spinning in the aisles°.

A group of customers, who had witnessed° the scene, started clapping and cheering.

Glossary

- **aisles:** corridors between the shelves
- **at full speed:** very fast
- **raced:** ran quickly
- **shaving:** when a man takes the hair from his face
- **shoplifter:** someone who steals from shops
- **sprawling:** lying in a disordered way
- **took aim:** (here) decided where to kick
- **witnessed:** seen

'What is going on here?' said Mr Moore.

Gary stopped. He looked around him. Everything was a complete mess. There were cans of peas everywhere. Mr Moore stared at him. Gary felt his face turn red.

'I'm so sorry, Mr Moore,' he said. 'I promise you I'm leaving now and I won't come back. Please don't be angry. I'll clean up before I go.'

'Gary,' said Mr Moore, 'you were sensational•. I want you to stay!' Gary couldn't speak. He was so pleased and so relieved•.

Two policemen in a police car arrived just a few minutes after the incident. Then a reporter and a photographer arrived from the local newspaper. Ray handed the shoplifter over to the policemen. The man's overcoat was full of perfumes, aftershaves, and electric toothbrushes.

'Great shot,' said Ray. 'Maybe you can teach me how to do that.'

'Incredible,' said Karen. 'They need players like you at the Academy, Gary.'

She stopped. 'What time is that test? Did you say five o'clock?'

Gary looked at his watch. 'Oh no!' he said, 'It's a quarter to five. I've got to go.'

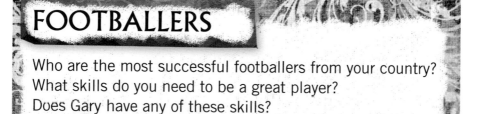

FOOTBALLERS

Who are the most successful footballers from your country?
What skills do you need to be a great player?
Does Gary have any of these skills?

Glossary

- **relieved:** he didn't feel worried or stressed
- **sensational:** wonderful; great

THE TEST

Gary and Karen ran all the way to the Academy. When they arrived it was already ten minutes past five.

'I'm sorry,' said a blonde woman at the door of the exam room. 'You're late and the test has already started.'

She looked at her notebook. 'You must be Gary,' she said. 'Everyone came on time. Why didn't you?'

'Please just give me one chance,' said Gary. 'Something happened. Really, it's not my fault.'

'It's true,' said Karen. 'You have to believe him. He's telling the truth.' Karen told her the story of the shoplifter. The woman's eyes opened wide as Karen described what had happened.

'And it will be in the newspapers tomorrow,' said Karen.

The woman thought for a moment.

'All right,' she said. 'But we can't give you any extra time. Take a place and don't disturb the others.'

Gary turned and looked at Karen. He mouthed the words•, 'Thank you' to her.

Gary looked at the test paper. His heart was pounding•. He remembered what Laura had told him. 'Stay calm. Read all the questions carefully first. Decide what questions you are going to answer, then work out how much time is available for each question. Make sure you save ten minutes for checking at the end.'

He had ninety minutes. He had to do a Maths paper and an English paper. Allowing ten minutes for checking, he had forty minutes for each paper. He set to work. He finished the Maths paper in twenty-five minutes. He thought about it. It was too easy. Maybe he had made a mistake. He checked his watch and started on the English paper. He scratched• his head. It wasn't easy. He answered all the questions and checked his watch from time to time. He finished the English paper in thirty-five minutes. Then he read his Maths paper again. He found one mistake. He was glad he had checked carefully. He checked his English paper. He found two grammar mistakes and three spelling mistakes. He made the corrections. He looked through all his answers one more time. He was satisfied. He took a deep breath and put down his pen. The room was quiet. He could only hear the sound of pages turning and pens writing. He checked his watch. He had finished fifteen minutes before the end of the test.

Glossary

- **mouthed the words:** mimed the words but did not say them
- **nodded:** moved his head up and down to say 'yes'
- **pounding:** beating fast and loudly
- **scratched his head:** moved his fingers up and down his head (see illustration)

When he gave his test paper to the blonde woman, she said,
'Are you sure you've finished?'
Gary nodded•. 'I did my best,' he said.

DO YOUR BEST

Think of a time when you did your best. Tell a partner.

Outside Gary found Karen sitting on the steps waiting for him.

'How long have you been here?' he said.

'Since you went into the exam room,' said Karen. 'How did it go?'

'I'm not sure,' said Gary.

Karen smiled. 'I'll keep my fingers crossed●,' she said.

At the Academy gates, parents waited for their children.

'Look who's here,' said Karen.

'Hello, stranger,' said a voice.

'Dad!' said Gary. 'What are you doing here?'

'Well, it's Sunday night. I don't have any interviews to go to, so I came here. I must say this is a very strange time to take a test.' He laughed. 'Let me take you and Karen for something to eat. You deserve it!'

'I'm starving●,' said Gary.

'Because you don't usually use up so much brain power,' said Karen.

'Careful, Karen,' said Gary, 'or you'll be in big trouble.'

'Now, what would you like to eat,' said Gary's dad. 'Pizza? Or would you prefer fish and chips?'

'Dad!' protested Gary.

'OK, only kidding!' said Dad. 'Come on. We've got a lot to talk about.'

Glossary

- **fingers crossed:** a way of wishing for luck
- **starving:** very hungry

The phone call came on Monday evening. Gary was helping Matt and Joe with their Maths homework and Karen was sitting on the sofa, reading a football magazine.

'It's for you, Gary,' said Mum, and she whispered, 'It's the Academy!'

Gary's heart was beating fast when he picked up the phone.

'Gary?' said a voice at the other end of the line. 'This is Mrs Dexter calling from the Football Academy. We've got the results of your test.'

Gary fell silent.

'Are you there, Gary?' said Mrs Dexter.

'Yes,' he said. 'Yes, I'm here.'

'Congratulations. You've passed,' she said. 'You did very well. In fact, you got the highest marks. We would like to offer you a place,' continued the woman. 'If you decide to take up the offer, you can come to our office any evening this week to sign up and pay your fees. The office opens at half past four.'

'I'll be there,' said Gary, 'and I won't be late!'

GREAT THANKS!...

MIAOW

After Reading

Personal Response

1 **Read each sentence and circle the number that is most true for you.**

1 = **absolutely not**
5 = **very much**

a) I liked the story.
  1   2   3   4   5
b) I had no problems in understanding the story.
  1   2   3   4   5
c) I now know many new words.
  1   2   3   4   5
d) I would recommend the book to a friend.
  1   2   3   4   5

2 **Were you surprised by the ending of the story? Did you expect it? Why/why not?**

3 **What is Gary like at the beginning of the story? How is he different at the end of the story?**

4 **What did you think of Gary? Do you think he will continue to work hard and be a good student at the Academy?**

5 **What is Gary's connection with the following characters?**
  a) Mr Page   b) Mr Steele   c) Mr Kumar

6 **What did you think about Gary's friends? Did they do enough to help Gary? Would you like to meet any of the characters from the story? Who?**

After Reading

Comprehension

1 Are the following sentences True (T) or False (F)? Tick (✔)

	T	F
a) The players from Manning High win the match at the beginning of the story.	☐	☐
b) Gary's father is looking for a new job.	☐	☐
c) Karen works as a tea lady for Manchester United.	☐	☐
d) Academy students have to attend coaching sessions four evenings a week and every Saturday.	☐	☐
e) Gary is sixteen years old.	☐	☐
f) Gary's parents can't afford to pay the Academy fees.	☐	☐
g) Laura is Karen's sister.	☐	☐
h) Gary doesn't like his job at the fish and chip shop.	☐	☐
i) Matt shows Gary how to fill the supermarket shelves.	☐	☐
j) Gary doesn't want to go to his lesson with Laura.	☐	☐
k) Rick destroys Gary's display of tuna.	☐	☐
l) Gary arrives late for work on his last day at the supermarket.	☐	☐
m) Gary gets a job as a babysitter.	☐	☐
n) Gary has one and a half hours to do the Maths and English tests.	☐	☐

2 Match the two halves of the sentences to sum up the story.

a) ☐ Gary is a teenager
b) ☐ Gary tries to get into the Academy
c) ☐ Karen, Joe and Matt find their friend
d) ☐ Gary loses his jobs
e) ☐ In the end Gary works hard and

1 because he is not prepared to make an effort.
2 a teacher and some part-time jobs.
3 who wants to become a professional footballer.
4 passes the Academy test with the highest marks.
5 but fails because his schoolwork is not good enough.

3 When does Gary say the following? Match with the situations below.

a) You have to be good at spelling and sums.

d) I did my best.

e) I got the goal. I hope you all saw that.

b) I promise I won't ever be late again.

c) Pay at the cash desk, please.

f) I'll pass the test and I'll get a job.

1 ☐ After he fails to get a free place at the Academy.
2 ☐ When he is working at the fish and chip shop.
3 ☐ After he takes the test at the Academy.
4 ☐ When he plays with the children in the park.
5 ☐ When he arrives at Laura's house for his lesson.
6 ☐ After the match with Manning High.

After Reading

Characters

1 The story's main character is Gary, a football-mad teenager. Who are the other characters in the story? How are they connected with Gary? Why are they important to the story? Work with a partner and make a chart like this:

Character	Connection	Importance
Laura	She is the older sister of Gary's friend Matt.	She helps Gary to prepare for his exam.

2 How does Gary feel in the following situations? Choose words from the box.

> stunned   annoyed   miserable   efficient   serious   irritated

a) When he arrives home after having an argument with Karen.

b) When Karen says that he is late for the appointment with Mr. Steele.

c) When he finds out that he didn't get a free place at the Academy.

d) When he tells his parents about the entry test and his decision to pay his own fees.

e) When he realizes he must study and go to work.

f) When it is his last day in the supermarket and he makes an effort to work hard.

3 Choose three adjectives that describe Gary at the beginning of the story.

> kind   lazy   thoughtless   hard-working   clever   stupid

....

Choose three adjectives that describe Gary at the end of the story.

....

4 Write the names of the characters beside the sentences.

a) He was a successful footballer but he hurt his knee playing in a game.

....

b) She loves football and she wins a place on the Crossbridge Football Academy training scheme.

....

c) He is a security guard at the Pricewise supermarket.

....

d) He is jealous of Gary and causes him a lot of trouble.

....

e) He is at school with Gary and his uncle owns a fish and chip shop.

....

5 Listen and number the pictures.

a)

b)

c)

d)

6 Imagine you're a newspaper reporter. A young footballer called Gary has caught a shoplifter at the supermarket where he works. What questions would you ask him? Ask and answer with a partner.

After Reading

Plot and Theme

1 What happens in the story? Put the events in the correct order.

1	2	3	4	5	6	7	8	9	10	11	12	13	14
a													n

a) Karen, Joe and Matt get free places on the Crossbridge Football Academy training scheme, but Gary does not.

b) On his last day at the supermarket, Gary makes a big effort to work hard.

c) Gary promises his parents he will pass the Academy test and get a job.

d) Gary's friends can't help him when he loses his job at the supermarket.

e) Gary learns from Mr Steele that he has low marks in English and Maths.

f) Gary starts a new job at the supermarket where Karen works.

g) Karen, Matt and Joe find Gary a job and a teacher.

h) Gary asks Laura to help him pass the test.

i) Gary gets into a fight with Rick at the fish and chip shop.

j) Gary catches a shoplifter by kicking a tin of beans under his feet.

k) Rick tells Gary he is a loser and Gary realizes that he has let his friends down.

l) Rick upsets Gary's display of tinned peas.

m) Mr Moore is pleased with Gary and invites him to continue working in the supermarket.

n) Gary arrives late for the Academy test, but he passes and gets the highest marks out of all the exam entrants.

2 **Tell the story in your own words. Use the plot events to guide you.**

3 **Imagine you are Karen. Write an email to a friend describing what happened to Gary and how you felt. Start anywhere in the story, or begin at the beginning, like this:**

> ● ○ ○
>
> Hi ....
> I've got some great news. I told you I applied to go to the Football Academy. Well, guess what? I got in! I can't believe it. I'm so happy. But… there's one big problem. The problem is Gary.

4 **At the end of the story, Gary says: 'I'll be there, and I won't be late!'**
   Work with a partner and make some predictions about what will happen to Gary when he starts his training at the Crossbridge Football Academy.

5 **Develop the plot. Work with a partner.**
   Decide what will happen to Rick.
   Will he continue to make Gary's life difficult?
   What about Gary's dad? Do you think he will be able to find a job?

6 **What are the themes of the story?**
   Discuss in groups and think of situations when you had similar experiences.

After Reading

Exit Test

1 **Listen and choose the correct picture.**

a) What does Gary take from Rick?

1 ☐

2 ☐

3 ☐

b) Where does Gary tell the boys to run?

1 ☐

2 ☐

3 ☐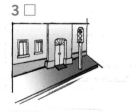

c) Where has Gary put the washing-up liquid?

1 ☐

2 ☐

3 ☐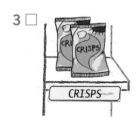

d) Where was Gary yesterday?

1 ☐

2 ☐

3 ☐

2 **Read the sentences about the story and choose the best word (1, 2 or 3) for each space.**

a) The main character in the story is a teenager who is

.... but lazy.

   1 happy   2 quiet   3 ambitious

b) When Gary doesn't get a place on the Academy course he is very

....

   1 angry   2 disappointed   3 pleased

c) Gary's friends find him .... jobs.

   1 three   2 two   3 four

d) Gary lost his job at the fish and chip shop because he

....

   1 was late   2 started a fight   3 made mistakes

e) Gary takes lessons with Laura and discovers that he is good at

....

   1 History   2 English   3 Maths

f) Gary helped to catch ....

   1 a reporter   2 a shoplifter   3 a goalkeeper

3 **Look at the picture on page 51 with a partner. Ask and answer questions about it.**

After Reading

Projects

1 Famous Footballers

This is Theo Walcott. He is one of Britain's best young footballers. He won his first sponsorship deal with Nike when he was just 14 and he went to play for Southampton senior side when he was 15. He is the youngest-ever player to play for England – he played for England against Hungary when he was 17.

Find out about Theo and fill in the fact file below

Name	....
Date of Birth	....
Place of Birth	....
Current Team	....
Position	....
First Premiership Goal	....
International Matches	....
Hobbies	....
Favourite Team	....

2 Make a fact file for your favourite footballer.

3 What sport are you passionate about? Search for information about it on the Internet. Are there academies where you can improve your performance in your favourite sport? Design your own academy.